Waiting

Waiting

Poems by

Suzanne Kamata

© 2022 Suzanne Kamata. All rights reserved.
This material may not be reproduced in any form, published,
reprinted, recorded, performed, broadcast,
rewritten or redistributed without
the explicit permission of Suzanne Kamata.
All such actions are strictly prohibited by law.

Cover design by Shay Culligan

Cover photo by Vicky Sim at Unsplash.com

ISBN: 978-1-63980-072-8

Kelsay Books
502 South 1040 East, A-119
American Fork, Utah 84003
Kelsaybooks.com

For Shari and Debra.
R.I.P.

Acknowledgments

These poems were originally published as a novella-in-verse
in the online journal *YARN*

Contents

Waiting	11
Vigil	12
Shira	13
Her Voice	14
Monday Afternoon	15
What My Mother Sees	17
60%	18
The Boyfriend	19
Yellow Ribbons	20
Next Year	21
Locks	22
Outside	23
Headlines	24
Her Beautiful Sister	25
The Search	26
One Evening	27
One Night	28
"No"	30
Going Out	31
At the All Ages Club	33
The Next Morning	34
Part-time Job	35
Questions	36
Trapped	37
Two Weeks Later	38
Two Roads	40
Running	41
Among the Pines	42
What the Breeze Brings	43
Benjamin	44

Waiting

My brother Benjamin waits
for Gent
our lost cocker spaniel
to come home.

Dad waits
for his boss
to give him a promotion.

Mom waits
for portents
and signs.

My boyfriend waits
for me to say
"yes."

I wait
for the future
far away from
here.

The town waits
for a missing girl
to turn up and tell us
it was all just a joke.

Vigil

My little brother Benjamin
fills the plastic dish
only to later dump
the untouched nuggets
and fill the dish
again, a ritual
a sacrificial offering
to our lost Cocker Spaniel.

He's gone door to door
promising mown lawns
washed windows
shined cars
in exchange for information.
No one helps.
Everyone is more concerned about
the disappearance of a young woman.

Young women disappear
with alarming regularity.
Two dead, in the woods
naked.
A third
still missing.
Shira Bates.

Shira

I was invited to her birthday party
in kindergarten.
I tried to wrap up
my mother's engagement ring
after snatching it from a crystal saucer
while she washed dishes
a suitable gift for such a princess of a girl
I thought.

Mom caught me
spanked my behind
made me give Shira a Barbie
with silky blonde hair
smooth skin

wearing the latest fashions
like the birthday girl herself.

I was more Raggedy Ann.

Later, Shira and I drifted apart.
She fell in with the cheerleaders
became star of the chorus
girlfriend to Number One Hottie
Greg Shealy
found God.

While I faded into
gawkiness
good grades
and hid behind glasses
and my long stringy hair.

Invisible me.

Her Voice

On the last day of school
a week before she went missing
Shira Bates sang with the chorus in
the school cafeteria
while I ate my blueberry yogurt.

Her voice blended then
soared above, the others went
silent, listening to her solo before
jumping back in again.

That girl could sing angels out of
the sky, could get larks to land on
her outstretched hands, I thought with
a kind of wonder instead of the usual
jealousy that I felt around Shira Bates.

Monday Afternoon

The phone rings.
It's Brian, I know
same time
every day
three rings
till Mom picks up.

Brian, at his summer job
calling to complain about
the heat
his boss
how much he hates construction work.

Brian wants
law school
his father's practice
his life all planned out
two-car garage
a Porsche for weekends
swimming pool
golf club
two kids—a boy and a girl
wife
(maybe me)

When he calls
he doesn't say
"How are you?"
"What do you want?"
"What shall we do tomorrow night?"

He doesn't know
what I eat for breakfast
or my favorite color
or what I want to be when
I grow up.

When he graduates
I'll be far away
in the Peace Corps
or
backpacking through Southeast Asian jungles
or
teaching English in a refugee camp somewhere
Anywhere
but
here.

What My Mother Sees

The images come to her
like light
bright flashing blinding
bolts of truth.

A car overturned
on the bypass
a severed limb
the unblinking eyes
of a corpse.

A barefoot child
stumbling over shards
of broken glass.

"What did you see this time?"
I ask my mother.

"You" she says
and shudders.
She won't tell me
the rest.

60%

Sometimes my mother is wrong.
She predicted that Benjamin
would break his arm
the day before he fell
out of his treehouse
but she couldn't see
my SAT scores
or what my homeroom teacher
would write on my letter of recommendation
for my college application.
She doesn't know if I will get into
Duke
or Yale
or Brown
so I cross my fingers
and hope.

The Boyfriend

The first time I saw him
my knees melted
butterflies flurried
in my stomach.

He asked me out
even though Melissa
is thinner and Laura
is funnier and Clara
has blonde hair
down to her waist.
He asked me
plain old me.

"What did you see in me?"
I asked him one time.
"I like you" he said
"because you seem just out
of reach."
And he held my hand
tighter
than
before.

Yellow Ribbons

Everyone along our street has tied
a yellow ribbon to
their mailbox post.
It means
"Shira, come home safely."

By day
volunteers hold hands
make a human chain
walk through field and forests.

Dogs sniff her clothes
try to pick up her scent.

At night
we gather
light candles
pray.

Next Year

He says
maybe we'll both go to
the University of South Carolina
and we'll tailgate at
football games

GO COCKS!

and play Frisbee on the quad
and head for one of those
houses on stilts at the beach
during spring break and you'll
join a sorority and I'll join
a frat and pin you.

Like a butterfly?
Maybe not.

Locks

Dad adds deadbolts to all the doors
that had double locks already.
He has an alarm system
installed, talks about getting
a new dog
not a cuddly family pet
like Gent
but a barking, snarling beast
a pit bull
a German shepherd
an animal that will
protect us.
Our house has become
a fortress. Indoors
we feel safe from
lightning strikes
drunk drivers
killers of young women.

"But Dad," I say
"Shira Bates wasn't in her house.
She was outside
at the edge of her driveway
getting the mail."
"See?" he says.
"It's better to stay
inside."

Outside

Beyond the walls of our house
is the forest of pine
other houses
churches, bars, schools
and the city
the University of South Carolina
the club where I go dancing
the restaurant where I tend the salad bar
the state capital building with
stars marking Civil War bullets
Confederate flag waving out front.

Beyond that, other cities
Orangeburg
Charleston
and the ocean
teeming with
dolphins, whales, sea turtles
schools of shimmery fish
darting among
shipwrecks
mysteries beneath the waves
that lap onto other shores
France
one of the places that I long to visit.
That I will visit.

Headlines

The Braves lost
in baseball
7-3.

A house
went up in flames
3 people
dead.

The pope
will be visiting
even though this state
is 80% Protestant
only 15% Catholic.

Streets will be
blocked off.

No news about Shira
is
             good
                           news?

Her Beautiful Sister

Krissie started out as Little Miss Chitlin' Strut
in a poufy pink dress
graduated to Miss Peach Blossom
wreathed in fragrant flowers
Vaseline on her teeth
then became Miss South Carolina
and finally, runner-up to
Miss America herself.

We saw her crying on TV.

Most people look ugly when they sob
but her tears shimmered
like diamonds.

Now there are no tears
as she looks into the camera
presses her hands together
says
"Whoever you are
I beg you
please don't hurt my sister
Shira."

The Search

The police combed
the mall
the woods
the schoolgrounds.

The cops questioned
her ex-boyfriend
the man in the house with the vicious dog
her classmates.

Hours went by
                days
a week
Finally the kidnapper called.

One Evening

Dad finally gets bumped up
to Director of Sales.
To celebrate
his coworkers throw him a party
dinner
cash bar
adults only.

One Night

Mom and Dad go out.
I get babysitting duty.
Brian comes over "to help."
I tuck in my little brother
with his stuffed Cocker Spaniel
a replica of Gent
listen to his prayers:
"Please God, help him
find his way home."
Read him a story about
a dog named Lassie
turn off the light
kiss him
leave the room
go back to Brian,
on the sofa
shove away his grabby hands
watch TV.

Twenty minutes later a door opens

I hear Benjamin cough.
"You're supposed to be asleep, kid."
He rubs his eyes
yawns
nods.
"I know. I'm trying."
I give him a glass of milk
a cookie
a different pillow
another story.

"Maybe I should go outside and wait," he says.
"No, it's too late for that," I say.
"I just heard something."
I hear it, too
a scraping sound
like branches on window glass
or fingernails.

I check the locks.
Bolted.
I turn on the porch light.
Nothing there.
"It's probably just the wind," I say.
Does he believe me?
Do I believe me?
I let him watch old movies on TV with
Brian and me until he falls asleep.

"No"

"Please,"
he says.
"We're gonna get married anyway.
Some day.
Aren't we?"

His breath is hot on my neck.
His fingers are like spiders
crawling
everywhere.

I push his hands away.
"Not yet."
I'm not ready

"Wait," I tell him.

He huffs
gets up from the sofa
yanks on his T-shirt
heads for the door.
"I need to cool off.
I'll call you later."

I stay on the sofa
listen to the door creak
           then slam
the roar of his car's engine
peal of tires
and then uneasy silence.

Going Out

"Where are you headed
dressed like that?"
my father asks.

I'm wearing
a short black skirt
fishnet stockings
pink tank top
Doc Martens
strands of fake pearls.
"Dancing," I tell him. "With my friends."
Just girls. No boyfriends.

At the all-ages club downtown
we can lose ourselves in
waves of sound
whirling bodies
drumbeats   heartbeats   strobes of light
forget about everything.

"Throw a jacket on,"
he grumbles.
Sure, Dad.
It's 90 degrees outside.

"See you later."
I jingle my keys.
Sound effects
bring Mom into the room
her eyes all wild.

"Take my car," she says,
handing me her keys.

"Why?
Your car eats gas.
It's hard to park.
It doesn't have a decent stereo."

"Please."
She presses the keys
into my palm
toothy ridges imprinting
on my flesh.
"I had a vision last night.
I saw you
in your car
so awful."

I don't say anything
can't think of words
only prickles.
I'm tired of living in fear.

I take her keys
kiss her on the cheek
stamp out the door
step past Benjamin on the steps.
Still waiting.

At the All Ages Club

Surrounded by friends
I let myself fall
into the music
nothing exists
except the beat
against my breastbone
the songs making me spin
loose
carefree
until I re-emerge
into the darkness of reality

The Next Morning

I wander into the kitchen dazed ears still muffled by last
night's loud music, seeking breakfast.
I swing open the refrigerator door
peer inside
pickles   mustard   olives
plastic containers of week-old food
nothing that I want.

Mom waves the newspaper in my face.
"They found her," she says.

"Who? What? Where's the orange juice?"

"They found her out in the woods
her clothes hanging from a tree."

"What are you talking about?"

"Shira Bates."

I set the door free
let it slam shut.

I squeeze my eyes shut.
Shira Bates
is
dead.
Gent
has been missing
for nine days.
There is
no
orange
juice.

Part-time Job

I work the salad bar at Shoney's
with Cora who's doing time for
writing bad checks
now out on the prison release program.

Cora knows someone who
knows someone who knows
someone on the police force.
Rumor has it
Shira's body was found
in the woods wrapped
in plastic, a mummy.

Questions

Did Shira say "no"?
Did she pray?
Did she try to escape?
Did she think of her dog?
Did she shout for her mother? Greg Shealy? For God?
Did she think she would be rescued?
Did she get to choose her last meal?
Did she try to reason with her kidnapper?
Did she feel cold?
Did she feel scared?
Hungry?
Did she think about that one time when she sang
in the school cafeteria and we all gave her a standing ovation?
Did she know she was going to die?

Trapped

Inside the house
a prisoner
I want to scream.
I need to get out of here
be alone
me, only me
away from the clatter of dishes
the drone of the TV
the six o'clock news
Mom's voice, insistent as a
mosquito.

Two Weeks Later

After dinner I put on my running shoes.
Mom watches me tie the laces
frowns.

"What are you doing? Where are going?"

"For a run."

"Where?"

"I don't know. Around."

"It's not safe.
Some creep could come
along in a pick-up
grab you like…"

"I AM GOING FOR A RUN!"
Mom sighs.
"Okay, you're old enough
to ignore the wisdom
of your elders, but take this."
A can of mace.
"And for God's sake,
be careful."

I grab the mace
leave it behind
a potted plant when she's not looking.

I pass Benjamin
waiting on the steps
as usual
think of inviting him
along, ruffle his hair instead.

His smile is brave
full of hope
as he sits next to the dog
food dish, freshly filled.

Two Roads

One way leads to
a subdivision
lawns with sprinklers
barking dogs
kids on bikes
People to wave at
nod to
talk with.

The other way leads to
sprawling farms with
wide open fields
cows on hills
acres of pines
forest but not those woods.

I choose the cows.

Running

My mind goes blank
feet crunch stones
pieces of my self cometogether.
Nothing but
        breath
                        movement
        heartbeat.

I hold out my hand.
Pine needles brush my palm.
NO TRESSPASSING
signs aren't for me
but for Hansels and Gretels trailing
soda cans and gum wrappers
idiots
with no respect for nature.

Birds call me
into the woods.

Among the Pines

I leap over logs
each footfall cushioned
by piles of pine needles.
Away from the road
I slow down
sigh
sit down
on the ground
take off my shoes
feel the moss with my toes
watch an ant trek across my leg
fascinated.

What the Breeze Brings

But then a gentle wind
stirs up leaves and a horrible
odor drifts over to
me until the whole forest
smells like rotten meat, decay.

I try not to breathe
I have to
I'm gasping
panicking
as I fumble with shoes
with steps.
Back on my feet I burst through forest
branches scratch at my arms
I slip
fall
ignore the blood on my knee
start running
toward the edge of the forest
toward light
toward the road.

Then I see flies buzzing above
bones, scraps of flesh
I choke back a sob and fall to
my knees. All that is left intact is
the collar that encircled his neck.

Tears cloud my vision as I claw at
earth digging up pine needles and dirt
to cover him. I build a mound, a grave
a tribute to our lost Cocker Spaniel
get back up on my feet and run home.

Benjamin

"Why are you crying?"
my little brother asks
when I come up the driveway.

I bend down
wrap my arms around him
hold him tight.
He squirms in
my sweaty embrace
nearly suffocating
against my shoulder
but he pats my back
awkwardly
lovingly.

I let go
look at his face
his shiny eyes filled with faith.
"What's wrong?" he asks softly.
Baby brother.
Little man.

"Nothing," I say. "Don't worry."
And then I sit down next to him
to wait. We sit there waiting
for Gent to come
home.

-end-

About the Author

Suzanne Kamata attended Lexington High School with Sharon Faye "Shari" Smith, who was murdered in 1985 by Larry Gene Bell. This crime compelled the writing of "Waiting." Kamata has also written several novels in prose, including Losing Kei (Leapfrog Press, 2008); Screaming Divas (Simon & Schuster, 2014); and The Baseball Widow (Wyatt-Mackenzie Publishing, 2021). She has a B.A. from the University of South Carolina and an M.F.A. from the University of British Columbia. She lives in Tokushima Prefecture, Japan, where she works as an associate professor at Naruto University of Education.

www.ingramcontent.com/pod-product-compliance
Lightning Source LLC
Chambersburg PA
CBHW060504110426
42738CB00055B/2652